Growing Food

Claire Llewellyn

SIMON & SCHUSTER

LONDON • SYDNEY • NEW YORK • TOKYO • SINGAPORE • TORONTO

Notes for parents and teachers
This book has a theme that threads its way through the topic. It does not aim to deal with the topic comprehensively; rather it aims to provoke thought and discussion. Each page heading makes a simple statement about the illustration which is then amplified and questioned by the text. Material in this book is particularly relevant to the following sections of the National Curriculum for England and Wales:

English: AT1 levels 1–2, AT2 levels 1–3
Geography: AT2 level 2, AT4 level 2
History: AT1 level 1 (sequencing of events)
Science: AT1 levels 1–3, AT2 levels 1–3, AT3 levels 1–3,
  AT5 level 2; AT16 level 1
Technology: AT4 level 2 (evaluating)

In Scotland the proposals of the Scottish Education Department apply.

TAKE ONE has been researched and compiled by Simon & Schuster Young Books. We are very grateful for the support and guidance provided by our advisory panel of professional educationalists in the course of the production.

Advisory panel:
Colin Pidgeon, Headteacher
Wheatfields Junior School, St Albans
Deirdre Walker, Deputy headteacher
Wheatfields Junior School, St Albans
Judith Clarke, Headteacher
Grove Infants School, Harpenden

British Library Cataloguing in Publication Data
Llewellyn, Claire
  Growing food.
  1. Food crops
  I. Title II. Series
  631

ISBN 0–7500–0595–5

Series editor: Daphne Butler
Design: M&M Design Partnership
Photographs: ZEFA except pages 8, 9, 13, 15BR, 18 Photos Horticultural and pages 19, 20 Harry Smith.
Line artwork: Raymond Turvey

First published in Great Britain in 1991 by Simon & Schuster Young Books

Simon & Schuster Young Books
Simon & Schuster Ltd
Wolsey House, Wolsey Road
Hemel Hempstead, Herts HP2 4SS

© 1991 Simon & Schuster Young Books

Printed and bound in Great Britain by BPCC Paulton Books Ltd

Contents

6

Fresh food tastes good

Have you ever picked fresh fruit
or vegetables?   What did you pick?
Did you have to bend low or stretch
high?   Did you get scratched?

Did you eat anything?   Can you
remember how it tasted?

Most plants grow from seeds

Seeds need to be wet and warm before they will grow.

Look at the seeds in these pictures.
How are they different from each other?
Can you think why some seeds are planted in trays?

9

Young plants need care

The seeds will soon grow into tiny plants.   They need water and warmth, and they also need light now to keep growing strongly.

The plants in the pictures have been spaced out.   Can you think why?

Protecting your plants

Birds, animals and insects will all enjoy eating your plants.   What do you think ate the apple in the picture?

Can you think of any ways to protect plants?   What might happen if you didn't protect them at all?

13

Which parts do we eat?

Most plants grow roots, a stalk,
leaves, flowers and seeds.
Sometimes the seeds are inside a fruit.

These foods all grow on plants.
Can you say which part of the plant
they are?

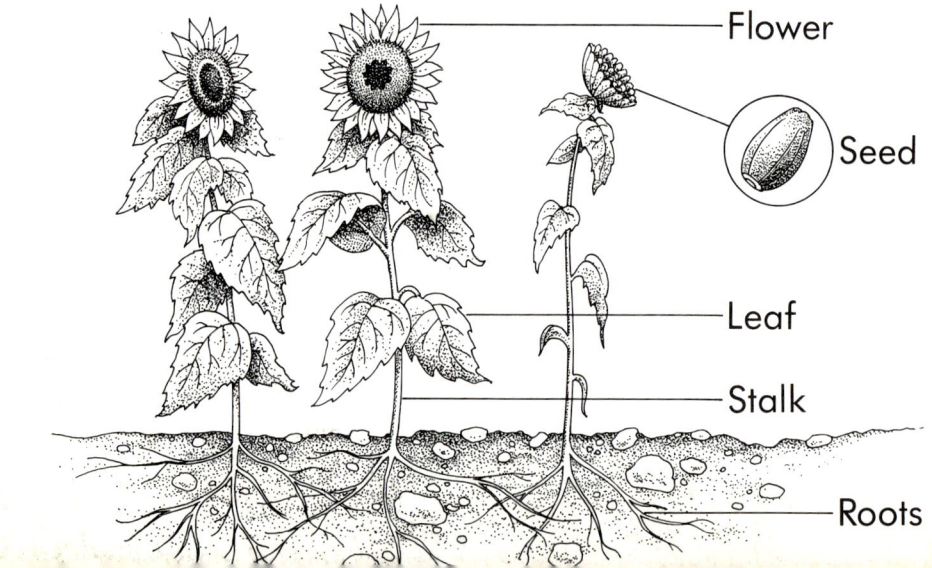

Flower

Seed

Leaf

Stalk

Roots

14

15

Plants need food too

A plant is a living thing, just like you.
It needs food and water to grow.
Some of its food comes from
the ground it grows in – the soil.

If you want good, strong plants
you need to feed the soil.

Can you think what might happen
to the soil if you grew too many plants
in a small space?

Feeding the soil

The green bin is called a compost.
If you pile dead leaves and plants
in it, they begin to go mushy.
What is in the other picture?

Both these piles of muck feed the soil.
How do we use them to do this?

19

20

Hand tools

If you want to grow food, you need special tools.

Do you know the names of all the tools in the picture?   What job does each one do?

What are the tools made of?
Can you think why?

Machines on the farm

Some farmers buy big, expensive machines to dig the soil, sow the seed and harvest the crops.

Sometimes animals are better than machines.   Can you think why?

23

Some crops need the sun

Plants grow and ripen in different seasons.

Think about where you live.   Which crops do the farmers grow in spring, summer, autumn and winter?

Look at the pictures.   Which of the crops do you think we can grow in this country?   Why can't we grow all of them here?

25

A good harvest

This farmer is harvesting his wheat.
Farmers always hope for a good
harvest from their crops.

Can you think of some reasons why a
harvest might fail?   What would
happen if there was no wheat?

Fresh food tastes good, but . . .

All these tomatoes are ripe. They
will be taken to shops and markets
all over the world.

Some of these tomatoes will be eaten
fresh. How will the others be used?
What happens to other sorts of fruit?

29

Index

animals 12, 22

birds 12

compost 18

crops 22, 24, 27

farmers 22, 24, 27

flowers 14

food 7, 14, 17, 18, 21, 28

fruit 7, 14, 28

harvest 22, 27

insects 12

leaves 14, 18